BE K...

by Kimberly M. Anderson

BE KIND

by Kimberly M. Anderson

© 2017 Kimberly M. Anderson

Illustrations by Jon Polen

Book Design & Production
Victor Driver, Sr.

Library of Congress Control Number: 2017912172

ISBN-13: 978-0692865347
ISBN-10: 0692865349

First Edition 2017

Published by
Kimberly M. Anderson, M.Ed., MS

In memory of my father
Mildrige (Andy) Anderson
"I love you to the moon and back."

Note to Parents

What can be more exciting than your child learning to develop social skills and enhancing their literacy skills in a fun way? Your child can improve their reading fluency and comprehension skills when they are encouraged by parents to read daily.

This book will introduce a variety of thoughts, feelings, and character-provoking social skills that may enhance your child's communication skills and instill timeless humanistic qualities.

This book is intended to teach and guide children about the importance of being kind, applying empathy and learning the true value of maintaining a healthy friendship.

Additionally, children will learn about expressing their feelings, being thoughtful, understanding the importance of respecting the feelings of others, being helpful, and learning appropriate ways to apply empathy and being helpful in social settings. These social skills can be learned, assessed, and applied by parents, teachers, and/or mental health professionals by completing the activities at the end of the story.

Table of Contents

Alaya and Zoey are best friends!
They have been friends since they could remember.

Everyday, while Alaya and Zoey are at school they play together.

Zoey likes to move her ring from hand to hand during recess.

10

They would hang out with each other all day and all night if they could.

11

During recess, Alaya and Zoey would go outside to dance.

A lot of the other kids like to play on the swings or have a game of basketball.

13

But not Alaya and Zoey.

When they hear music, they like to show each other their dance moves.

They like to jump up and down and shake it all around.

14

After dancing for five minutes, Zoey began to cry.

"Whats wrong, Zoey?" asked Alaya.

"I Can't find my ring,"
said Zoey.

17

"I will help you find your ring," said Alaya.

18

"We can go back to dancing after we find your ring."

Zoey and Alaya began to look for Zoey's ring.

"Zoey, we should check where we were last dancing!" said Alaya.

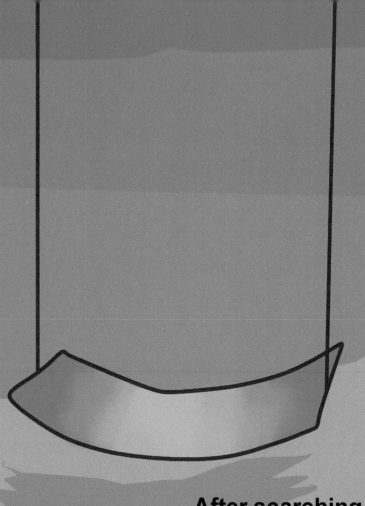

After searching the playground, Alaya found Zoey's ring by the swings.

"Thank you, Alaya,
for being a good friend!"

23

"You're welcome, Zoey! I help when I can.

That's what friends are for!"

Zoey and Alaya began dancing again.

Activities and Role Playing

Activity 1– Expressing Feelings

Activity Instructions:
We all have feelings. Feelings can range from being sad, happy, confused, disappointed, proud, surprised, and angry. In this activity children can act out their feelings as well as tapping into their emotions. These feelings can be acted out and expressed with parents, *teachers, and/or mental health professionals. Check the item once you have completed acting it out.*

1. Select a feeling that you experienced today: Draw a picture of that feeling.

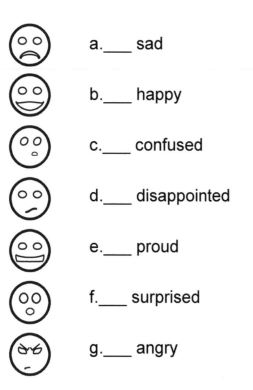

a.___ sad

b.___ happy

c.___ confused

d.___ disappointed

e.___ proud

f.___ surprised

g.___ angry

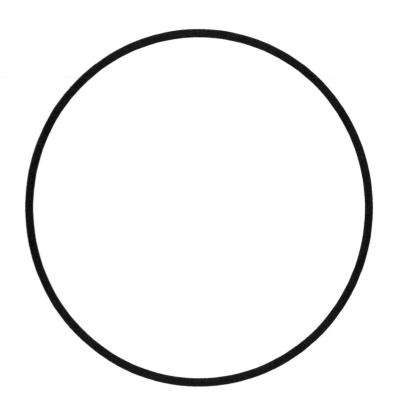

2. Act It Out!
Let's role play and act out each feeling! First, select a feeling shown on the previous page and allow for your child to identify and role play each feeling. Second, mime or show the expression of each feeling for them to guess.
Remember there is no wrong or right answer.

3. What feelings did Zoey display when she lost her ring? _____

_____

_____

_____

_____

Explore the feeling: _____

_____

_____

_____

_____

4. What made Alaya and Zoey happy? _____

_____

_____

Now explore what makes you happy? Explain. _____

_____

_____

_____

Activities and Role Playing

Activity 2– Being Helpful

Activity Instructions:

Everyone likes to be around a person that helps other people. Remember, anyone can help someone else. You can be big, little, tall, or short. In this book, Alaya is encouraged to help Zoey out when she lost her ring.

Answer each question to learn how you can be helpful at home and in your community. Remember there is no wrong or right answer.

1. There are many things you can do to be considered helpful. Check the box when you have completed each task.

❑ • Help an elderly person carry something from the grocery store.

❑ • Help your mom clean up your home.

❑ • Give your seat to an elderly person.

❑ • Help an elderly person cross the street.

2. Now think and list at least seven things that you can do to help others in your home or in your community.

1. _____

2. _____

3. _____

4. _____

5. _____

6. _____

7. _____

Activities and Role Playing

Activity 3– Empathy

Activity Instructions:
Empathy helps you put yourself in someone else's shoes. Basically, it is learning how someone else would feel about a situation. Answer each question to learn how empathy was displayed in the story and demonstrate how empathy can be shown to your friend.

Remember there is no wrong or right answer.

1. How do you think Alaya showed empathy to Zoey in the story? Explain.

_____

_____

_____

_____

_____

_____

_____

2. If you have a friend that was sad, how would you cheer them up? Explain.

_____

_____

_____

_____

_____

_____

Activities and Role Playing

Activity 4– The Value of Friendship

Activity Instructions:

Having a good friendship means keeping a healthy relationship between two people. Good friendships can be hard to come by. Being a good friend is doing something for a person that you would want them to do for you.

Answer each question to show what makes good character as a friend and how Alaya distributed good character as a friend throughout the story. Remember, there is no wrong or right answer.

1. What characteristic makes a good friend? Explain.

_____

_____

_____

_____

_____

_____

_____

2. How was Alaya a good friend to Zoey in this story? Explain. _____

_____

_____

_____

_____

_____

Literacy Activities

Comprehension Checklist

Think about what you have read in the story "Be Kind". Use the pictures in the story to help you find out the questions listed below.

Talk about what happened first in the story. _____

_____

_____

Then what happened next? _____

_____

_____

What happened at the end of the story? What was the problem in the story?

_____

_____

What was the most important idea in this book? _____

_____

Career Spotlight

What does an author do in a book? _____

What does an illustrator do in a book? _____

Using the Word "Kind" in a Word Web

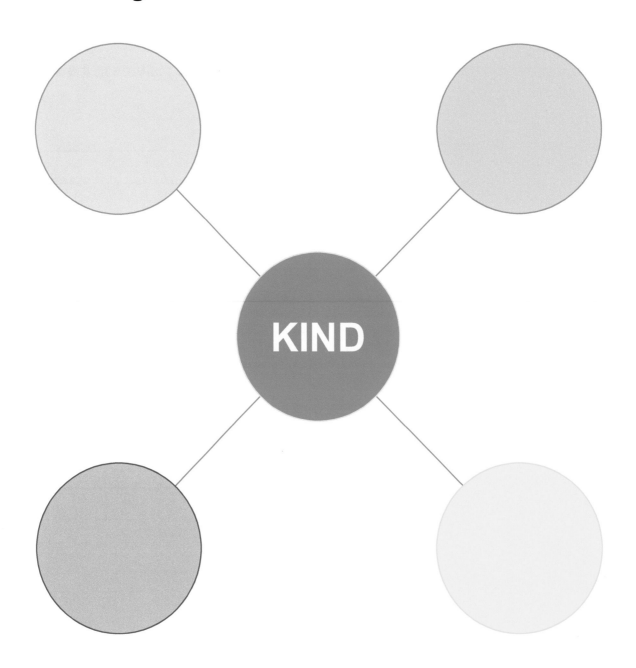

Fiction and Non-Fiction

Write something you might read in a non-fiction book about elephants and giraffes. Explain.

_____

_____

_____

_____

Write something you might read in a fiction book about elephants and giraffes. Explain.

_____

_____

_____

_____

Reading Fluency

Check My Fluency

Read the text highlighted and then copy each sentence three times.

They

They have

They have been

They have been friends

They have been friends since

They have been friends since they

They have been friends since they could

They have been friends since they could remember.

_____

_____

_____

Research

Use the internet or other books to help you learn more about Elephants and Giraffes.

What is something new that you did not know about an Elephant? _____

_____

_____

_____

_____

_____

_____

What is something new that you did not know about a Giraffe? _____

_____

_____

_____

_____

_____

_____

Glossary

(Words found in the Webster Dictionary)

angry – filled with anger: having a strong feeling of being upset or annoyed

characteristic – a special quality or trait that makes a person, thing, or group different from others

community – a group of people who live in the same area (such as a city, town, or neighborhood)

confused – unable to understand or think clearly

disappointed – feeling sad, unhappy, or displeased because something was not as good as expected or because something you hoped for or expected did not happen

empathy – the feeling that you understand and share another person's experiences and emotions; the ability to share someone else's feelings

feeling – an emotional state or reaction

friendship – the state of being friends; the relationship between friends

happy – feeling pleasure and enjoyment because of your life, situation, etc.

helpful – making it easier to do a job, deal with a problem, etc.; giving help

proud – very happy and pleased because of something you have done, something you own, someone you know or are related to, etc.; feeling pride

sad – affected with or expressive of grief or unhappiness

surprised – an unexpected event, piece of information, etc.

value – usefulness or importance

Contributors

Jon S. Polen, Illustrations

Jon S. Polen has lived in Oklahoma his entire life. He was born in the small town of Perry and now lives in Tulsa.

He graduated High School in Perry in 1985. He earned his Masters Degree in Rehabilitation Counseling at Langston University in Tulsa. His research interest includes, but not limited to: felons with physical disabilities, mental illness and substance abuse disorders, alternative sentencing and reintegration into workforce after incarceration. He has assisted in research and literature review relating to minority overrepresentation in the criminal and juvenile justice systems and transportation issues for persons with disabilities. He is currently a Licensed Professional Counselor and works with people from 3 to 99 years of age.

Victor Driver Sr, Book Design

Victor Driver, Sr. has been doing artwork since kindergarten. His desire to copy cartoons from the Sunday Comic Strips and his love of animated cartoons on Saturday mornings were his initial inspiration.

His education includes degrees in drafting and graphic design. Equipped with these skills, Driver produces professional graphics for just about any purpose.

As a fine artist, Driver enjoys pencil, colored pencil, pen & ink and watercolor. He also paints using acrylic and other mixed media.

His communication design career spans more than 35 years producing copy, ads, packaging, brochures, t-shirts, logos, and illustrations for clients across the U.S.A.

About the Author

Kimberly M. Anderson is the proud daughter of Mildrige and Rosie Anderson. Kimberly was born in Oklahoma City, Oklahoma and grew up in Midwest City, Oklahoma.

In 2001, she graduated from Midwest City High School. Kimberly is a very proud second generation graduate of Langston University where she earned a Master of Education in Elementary Education and a Master of Science in Rehabilitation Counseling. Ms. Anderson is currently a second grade teacher and mental health professional.

In her spare time, she often works with children, adolescents, and adults with behavioral/mental health concerns. Kimberly continues to focus her work and uplift children to teach them social skills and educate/advocate for women with Triple Negative Breast Cancer.